13

TRISKAIDEKAPHOBIA
BY ZEESHAN MAHMUD

WTF is Triskaidekaphobia?

Triskaidekaphobia is an irrational fear or aversion to the number 13. It is derived from the Greek words "tris" (meaning "three"), "kai" (meaning "and"), and "deka" (meaning "ten"), combined with "phobia" (meaning "fear"). People who suffer from triskaidekaphobia may avoid situations or circumstances involving the number 13 due to a belief in its unlucky or negative connotations. This fear can manifest in various ways, such as avoiding the 13th floor of buildings, refusing to participate in activities on Friday the 13th, or feeling anxious about dates or events associated with the number 13.

This aversion in Western culture, particularly in relation to Friday the 13th, and this superstition has roots in various historical and cultural contexts, including Norse mythology and Christian beliefs. Some notable instances include buildings omitting the 13th floor, airlines avoiding labeling rows with the number 13, and people being cautious about scheduling important events on Friday the 13th. It's intriguing how deeply ingrained these superstitions can be in society!

Cases of Places Avoiding the Number 13

The Curious Case of Mr. Schoenberg

There have been several famous people throughout history known to have triskaidekaphobia. One notable example is the composer Arnold Schoenberg, who allegedly feared the number 13 to the extent that he would avoid it whenever possible. He would often refer to it as "the devil's number" and even went as far as to rename his opera from "Moses und Aron" to "Moses und Aaron" to remove the offending number. It's intriguing to see how such fears can affect even the most accomplished individuals!

Arnold Schoenberg, the influential Austrian composer and music theorist, is said to have had a fear of the number 13, a condition known as triskaidekaphobia. Schoenberg's fear of the number 13 was particularly notable in his life and work, leading to several superstitious behaviors and decisions.

One of the most famous instances of Schoenberg's triskaidekaphobia is related to his composition "String Quartet No. 13," also known as "String Quartet No. 4." Schoenberg became fixated on the number 13 during the composition process and incorporated elements of numerology into the piece. He structured the quartet using a compositional technique known as twelve-tone serialism, which assigns equal importance to all 12 pitches of the chromatic scale, effectively avoiding the use of the 13th pitch.

Additionally, Schoenberg was known to avoid the number 13 in his personal life. He reportedly refused to stay in hotel rooms with the number 13, avoided conducting or attending events on the 13th of the month, and was cautious about scheduling concerts or premieres on dates associated with the number 13.

Schoenberg's triskaidekaphobia is often cited as an example of how superstitions and irrational fears can influence the lives and creative output of even the most brilliant and rational individuals. Despite his groundbreaking contributions to music and composition, Schoenberg's fear of the number 13 remained a consistent presence throughout his life.

Fons et Origo*

Triskaidekaphobia's origins are a bit murky, but it's believed to have roots in various cultural and historical influences. One theory suggests that the fear of the number 13 may have originated from Norse mythology, where 12 gods were invited to a banquet in Valhalla, but the mischievous Loki crashed the party, making the total 13. Another theory ties it to Christian beliefs, with the Last Supper being attended by 13 individuals, including Jesus and his 12 disciples, with Judas being the 13th to arrive and betray Jesus. These cultural associations likely contributed to the superstition surrounding the number 13, giving rise to triskaidekaphobia over time. It's fascinating how these beliefs can become deeply ingrained in societies around the world, shaping behaviors and traditions for centuries.

*Aight I juss wanted to sound pretenshus

History of triskaidekaphobia

Tarot card games can be traced back to around 1450 with the Visconti-Sforza Tarot, where the Death card, consistently numbered 13 across various variants, symbolizes misfortune.

In 1781, Antoine Court de Gébelin discussed the significance of this card in the Tarot of Marseilles, noting the universally held belief that the number 13 was unlucky. Johann Gottlob Immanuel Breitkopf later affirmed this notion in 1784, stating that the tarot card numbered 13 represented death and misfortune.

The superstition of "thirteen at a table" has been documented since at least 1774, with Johann August Ephraim Götze suggesting a religious origin. He speculated that this fear stemmed from the Gospel passage where Jesus dined with his twelve disciples at the Last Supper, creating an aversion to the number 13.

In the 1890s, English-language sources popularized the idea that Judas, the disciple who betrayed Jesus, was the 13th to sit at the table during the Last Supper, further fueling the fear of 13. However, biblical accounts do not specify the seating arrangement.

Douglas Hill's 1968 retelling of a Norse myth added to the superstition, recounting a dinner party in Valhalla attended by 12 gods, with Loki as the 13th uninvited guest. In this tale, Loki orchestrates the death of Balder using a mistletoe-tipped arrow, reinforcing the ominous association with the number 13. Despite its widespread retelling, the original Prose Edda by Snorri Sturluson does not emphasize the number 13 in this context.

3 Notable Cases

The Last Supper: The association of the number 13 with bad luck is often traced back to the biblical story of the Last Supper, where Jesus dined with his 12 disciples, resulting in a total of 13 individuals. Judas Iscariot, the disciple who betrayed Jesus, is traditionally considered the 13th guest at the table.

Knights Templar: Legend has it that on Friday, October 13, 1307, King Philip IV of France ordered the arrest of hundreds of Knights Templar, accusing them of heresy and other crimes. This event further solidified the superstition surrounding Friday the 13th as an unlucky day.

Apollo 13 Mission: The Apollo 13 mission, launched on April 11, 1970, encountered a series of life-threatening technical malfunctions, leading to the famous phrase "Houston, we have a problem." Some superstitious individuals attributed the mission's troubles to the fact that it was the 13th mission in the Apollo program.

Famous cases of unfortunate events occurring on the 13th:

1. Friday the 13th, 1307 - The Templar Knights' Arrest: King Philip IV of France ordered the arrest of hundreds of Knights Templar on Friday, October 13, 1307. The Templar Knights were accused of heresy and other crimes, leading to their downfall and persecution.

2. Apollo 13 Mission: On April 13, 1970, the Apollo 13 mission to the moon encountered a critical failure in space, leading to a life-threatening situation for the astronauts aboard. The mission had to be aborted, and the crew faced numerous challenges before safely returning to Earth.

3. Benghazi Attack: On September 13, 2012, the U.S. diplomatic compound in Benghazi, Libya, was attacked by militants, resulting in the deaths of four Americans, including U.S. Ambassador J. Christopher Stevens. The incident sparked controversy and led to investigations into the handling of security at diplomatic facilities.

These events, occurring on the 13th, have contributed to the superstition surrounding the number and the day.

While many of these events may be coincidental and not directly caused by the date itself, they have contributed to the superstition surrounding this day. Some examples include:

1. Black Friday bushfires (1939): In Australia, devastating bushfires broke out on Friday, January 13, 1939. These fires were some of the worst in the country's history, resulting in significant loss of life and property.

2. Uruguay Air Force Flight 571 crash (1972): On Friday, October 13, 1972, a plane carrying a Uruguayan rugby team crashed in the Andes Mountains. The survivors faced extreme conditions,

including cold temperatures and starvation, before being rescued more than two months later.

3. Stock Market Crash (1989): On Friday, October 13, 1989, the stock market experienced a significant drop, often referred to as the "Friday the 13th Mini-Crash." This event added to the superstition surrounding the date in financial circles.

4. Costa Concordia Disaster (2012): On Friday, January 13, 2012, the cruise ship Costa Concordia ran aground off the coast of Italy, resulting in the deaths of 32 people and leading to one of the largest maritime salvage operations in history.

What's the deal with Friday though?

The association of Friday with the number 13 being unlucky has historical and cultural roots. One possible explanation comes from Christian tradition, particularly the Last Supper. According to the Bible, Jesus dined with his 12 disciples on the evening before his crucifixion, which is commonly referred to as the Last Supper. Judas Iscariot, who betrayed Jesus, is traditionally considered to be the 13th guest at the table, and the betrayal led to Jesus' crucifixion on Good Friday. This association of Friday with betrayal and unfortunate events may have contributed to the superstition surrounding the combination of Friday and the number 13. Additionally, in Norse mythology, Friday was considered an unlucky day due to its association with the goddess Frigg, who was associated with love and fertility but also with foreboding and doom. These historical and cultural influences have combined to create the superstition surrounding Friday the 13th as an unlucky day.

Celebrities and fear of thirteen

While it's not always easy to confirm celebrities' personal fears, some modern figures have openly expressed their discomfort with the number 13. Here are a few:

1. Taylor Swift: The pop superstar has famously expressed her superstition regarding the number 13. She was born on December 13th, and it's been reported that she considers it her lucky number, even writing it on her hand during performances. However, she also acknowledges its potential for being unlucky.

2. Stephen King: The prolific author known for his horror novels, including "The Shining" and "It," has a well-documented fear of the number 13. He has been quoted as saying, "I'm scared of the number 13, I always have been. To me, it's not an unlucky number. It's a number that's always been ominous."

3. Fergie: The singer and former member of the Black Eyed Peas, Fergie, reportedly has triskaidekaphobia. She has mentioned in interviews that she's afraid of the number 13 and avoids it whenever possible.

Events related to triskaidekaphobia:

On Friday, October 13, 1307, Philip IV of France ordered the arrest of the Knights Templar. While the number 13 was considered unlucky, Friday the 13th wasn't seen as ominous during that era. The misconception that the Knights Templar's arrest was linked to the superstitions surrounding Friday the 13th arose in the early 21st century and gained popularity through the novel The Da Vinci Code.

In 1881, a significant group of New Yorkers led by US Civil War veteran Captain William Fowler aimed to dispel such superstitions. They established a dinner cabaret club, the Thirteen Club, convening for their inaugural meeting on January 13, 1881, at 8:13 p.m. Thirteen individuals gathered in Room 13 of the venue, walking under a ladder and dining amid spilled salt. Thirteen Clubs proliferated across North America over the next 45 years, attracting widespread attention and even counting five future US presidents among their members, from Chester A. Arthur to Theodore Roosevelt. However, these clubs eventually waned due to declining interest.

The British submarine HMS K13 sank on January 29, 1917, during trials after diving with a hatch and vents open. Though 48 men were rescued, 32 sailors and civilian technicians perished. Renamed K22 after repairs, it was involved in multiple collisions with other submarines on February 1, 1918, resulting in the deaths of 103 men in what became known as the Battle of May Island. The subsequent British L-class submarine omitted the number L13.

Apollo 13 launched on April 11, 1970, at 13:13:00 CST and encountered an oxygen tank explosion on April 13 at 21:07:53 CST. Miraculously, it safely returned to Earth on April 17.

The Friday the 13th mini-crash occurred on October 13, 1989, causing a stock market crash.

In Ireland, concerns arose in 2012 among members of the Society of the Irish Motor Industry (SIMI) regarding vehicle registration plates bearing the number 13. Fear of superstition affecting car sales prompted the government, in collaboration with SIMI, to modify the registration plates for 2013 to read "131" for vehicles registered in the first half of the year and "132" for the latter half.

History of the 13th Club in New York

The Thirteen Club, also known as The Thirteen Club of New York, was a group formed in the late 19th century with the aim of debunking superstitions surrounding the number 13. The club's activities and gatherings were designed to challenge common superstitions and show that the number 13 was not inherently unlucky.

Here are some more details about the history and activities of The Thirteen Club:

1. Formation: The Thirteen Club was founded in 1881 by Captain William Fowler, a Civil War veteran, who was intrigued by superstitions surrounding the number 13. He believed that these superstitions were baseless and wanted to prove that the number was not unlucky.

2. Membership: The club consisted of 13 members, deliberately chosen to match the number considered unlucky. Members included prominent individuals from various fields, such as politics, business, and the arts. Some notable members included Ulysses S. Grant, Theodore Roosevelt, and Mark Twain.

3. Activities: The club's activities included regular dinners held on the 13th day of the month, where 13 people would sit down to a meal together. The table would be adorned with items considered unlucky, such as open umbrellas, broken mirrors, and spilled salt. Members would deliberately engage in actions believed to bring bad luck, such as walking under ladders or breaking mirrors, to challenge superstitions.

4. Success: The Thirteen Club gained attention and popularity for its unconventional approach to superstition. Its activities were covered by newspapers, and the club's message of skepticism towards superstitions resonated with many people. The club's success contributed to a broader cultural shift towards questioning traditional beliefs and superstitions.

5. Legacy: While The Thirteen Club eventually disbanded, its legacy lives on in the continued fascination with superstitions and the number 13. The club's activities helped to challenge and dispel common superstitions surrounding the number, paving the way for a more rational and skeptical approach to beliefs.

Overall, The Thirteen Club played a significant role in challenging superstitions and promoting critical thinking, leaving behind a lasting legacy in the history of skepticism and rationalism.

Triskaidekaphobia in sports!

In the realm of sports, there are athletes who either avoid or embrace the number 13 on their jerseys:

Avoiding Number 13:

1. Wilt Chamberlain: The legendary NBA player famously avoided the number 13 throughout his career. He wore number 13 only during his rookie season with the Philadelphia Warriors but switched to number 14 for the rest of his career.

2. Kurt Warner: The former NFL quarterback, known for his success with the St. Louis Rams and Arizona Cardinals, avoided wearing number 13 during his career. He chose numbers 13 and 10, depending on team availability, during his high school and college football years, but he didn't wear it in the NFL.

Embracing Number 13:

1. Dan Marino: The Hall of Fame NFL quarterback embraced the number 13 throughout his illustrious career with the Miami Dolphins. Despite some superstitions surrounding the number, Marino wore it proudly and achieved great success on the field.

2. Alex Rodriguez: The former MLB player, known as A-Rod, embraced the number 13 throughout his career with the Seattle Mariners, Texas Rangers, and New York Yankees. He

wore number 13 for much of his career and had some of his most notable achievements while wearing it.

Triskaidekaphobia in cards and numerology

1. The Curse of the King of Hearts: In some traditions, the King of Hearts is sometimes referred to as the "suicide king" because the positioning of his sword in the card appears to pierce his head. This association with death has led to superstitions surrounding the King of Hearts, particularly when it appears as the 13th card in a tarot deck or a standard deck of playing cards.

2. The Unlucky 13th Card in Tarot: In tarot card readings, the 13th card of the Major Arcana is often associated with transformation, death, and rebirth. This card, known as Death, does not necessarily signify physical death but rather represents endings and transitions. However, its appearance in a reading can evoke fear and anxiety due to its ominous symbolism.

3. The 13 of Spades in Russian Folklore: In Russian folklore, the 13 of Spades is sometimes referred to as the "card of death." It is believed that if this card is drawn from the deck, it foretells misfortune or even death for the person who drew it. This superstition has led to the 13 of Spades being considered unlucky in Russian culture.

These anecdotes showcase the cultural significance and superstitions surrounding card number 13, both in traditional playing card games and in other divinatory practices like tarot card readings.

In various fields such as numerology, Kabbalah, and other esoteric studies, the number 13 holds significance and symbolism beyond mere superstition. Here's a brief overview of how the number 13 is viewed in these disciplines:

1. Numerology: In numerology, the number 13 is often associated with transformation, rebirth, and regeneration. It is seen as a number of upheaval and change, representing the end of one cycle and the beginning of another. This transformational aspect of the number 13 can be both challenging and liberating, depending on how it is interpreted.

2. Kabbalah: In Kabbalistic teachings, the number 13 is associated with the concept of unity and harmony. It represents the idea of transcending the material world and achieving spiritual wholeness. In the Tree of Life, a central symbol in Kabbalah, the 13th sephira (or sphere) is often associated with the divine aspect of unity, where all aspects of existence converge.

3. Astrology: In astrology, the number 13 is associated with the planet Neptune. Neptune is often seen as a planet of illusion, intuition, and spiritual awakening. The number 13 may symbolize the mysterious and unseen forces at work in the universe, inviting individuals to explore the depths of their psyche and spiritual journey.

4. Tarot: In tarot card readings, the 13th card of the Major Arcana is often associated with transformation and change. The card Death, despite its ominous name, represents endings and new beginnings, signifying the completion of one phase of life and the start of another. It encourages

individuals to embrace change and let go of what no longer serves them.

While there aren't specific references to the 13th card being universally lucky or unlucky, individual interpretations and cultural beliefs may vary. In some traditions, the King cards are associated with power, authority, and success, which could be viewed as positive attributes. However, in other contexts or superstitions, the number 13 itself may be considered unlucky, leading to negative connotations associated with the 13th card.

In tarot card readings, the 13th card of the Major Arcana is the Death card. Despite its ominous name, the Death card symbolizes transformation, endings, and new beginnings rather than literal death. It encourages individuals to embrace change and let go of what no longer serves them, suggesting a more nuanced interpretation of the number 13 beyond mere superstition.

Number 13 in other cultures

There are several cultures where number 13 is considered lucky. Here are a few examples:

1. Italy: In Italian culture, the number 13 is generally considered lucky. The expression "fare tredici" ("to do 13") means to hit the jackpot or have a stroke of luck. Some Italians even regard Friday the 13th as a lucky day.

2. China: In Chinese culture, the number 13 is often considered lucky because it sounds similar to the word for "definitely" or "assuredly" (shí sān), which implies a guarantee of prosperity or success.

3. Japan: In Japanese culture, the number 13 is generally considered lucky. In fact, in Japanese traditions, the coming of age celebration called "Seijin no Hi" is held when a person turns 13 years old.

4. India: In Hindu culture, the number 13 is associated with prosperity and blessings. It is considered auspicious in many regions of India and is often included in rituals and ceremonies.

5. Mexico: In Mexican culture, the number 13 is considered lucky and is associated with good fortune. This belief is reflected in various aspects of Mexican life, including architecture, traditions, and folklore.

Story of the Number 13 Inn

In the year 1313, on the ominous 13th day of the month, which happened to fall on a Friday, young Thaddeus found himself wandering through the mist-shrouded streets of an ancient village. As the clock struck midnight, he stumbled upon an old inn, its weathered sign creaking in the chilly wind. The sign read "The Raven's Roost," and beneath it, in faded lettering, was the number 13.

Curiosity piqued, Thaddeus pushed open the heavy oak door and stepped into the dimly lit interior. The innkeeper greeted him with a solemn nod, his eyes betraying a hint of unease as they lingered on Thaddeus. Undeterred, Thaddeus requested a room for the night, and without a word, the innkeeper handed him the key to Room 13.

Ascending the creaky stairs to the 13th floor, Thaddeus couldn't shake the feeling of foreboding that hung heavy in the air. With each step, the shadows seemed to grow darker, and the silence more oppressive. Finally, he reached the end of the hallway and unlocked the door to Room 13.

As he entered the room, Thaddeus felt a chill run down his spine. The furnishings were sparse, and the air was thick with an otherworldly presence. Ignoring his growing unease, Thaddeus brushed it off as mere superstition and settled into bed.

But as the clock struck 1:13 a.m., strange things began to happen. Shadows danced across the walls, taking on eerie shapes that seemed to whisper ancient secrets. The temperature dropped, and Thaddeus could see his breath in the moonlight streaming through the window.

Suddenly, a low, guttural growl echoed through the room, freezing Thaddeus in place. Trembling, he glanced around frantically, searching for the source of the sound. That's when he saw it – a pair of glowing eyes, watching him from the darkest corner of the room.

Heart pounding, Thaddeus reached for the lantern on the bedside table, only to find it extinguished. In the pitch-black darkness, the eyes drew closer, their malevolent gaze fixed upon him. With a cry of terror, Thaddeus stumbled backward, his foot catching on something hidden in the shadows.

As he fell to the ground, Thaddeus's hand brushed against a hidden trapdoor, revealing a staircase leading down into the depths below. With no other choice, he descended into the darkness, the sound of his own frantic footsteps echoing off the stone walls.

What awaited Thaddeus in the depths of the inn's cellar, on that fateful Friday the 13th in the year 1313, remains a mystery lost to the annals of time. But one thing is certain – he would never forget the terror he experienced on that cursed night, in the 13th room of the Raven's Roost.

Reference of number 13 in movies

Other than the the 1999 movie *The Thirteenth Floor*, here are few cases where number 13 is mentioned din the title:

1. 13 Assassins (2010): Directed by Takashi Miike, this Japanese film follows a group of samurai who are tasked with assassinating a sadistic lord to prevent him from ascending to higher power.

2. 13 Going on 30 (2004): A romantic comedy starring Jennifer Garner and Mark Ruffalo, this film follows a 13-year-old girl who wakes up in the body of her 30-year-old self and must navigate adulthood while retaining her youthful spirit.

3. Thirteen (2003): Directed by Catherine Hardwicke, this drama explores the tumultuous relationship between a thirteen-year-old girl and her troubled best friend as they navigate adolescence and rebellion.

4. Ocean's Thirteen (2007): The third installment in the "Ocean's" film series, directed by Steven Soderbergh, this heist film follows Danny Ocean and his team as they plan and execute a complex casino heist in Las Vegas.

5. 13 Hours: The Secret Soldiers of Benghazi (2016): Directed by Michael Bay, this action thriller is based on the true story of the attack on the American diplomatic compound in Benghazi, Libya, and the heroic efforts of six security contractors who defended it.

The Story of the Cult of 13

In the shadowy depths of the forest, hidden from prying eyes, there lurked a sinister cult known only as the Cult of 13. For centuries, they had wielded their dark influence, worshiping the number 13 as a symbol of power and malevolence.

One stormy night, a man named Ethan, plagued by triskaidekaphobia, stumbled upon the cult's hidden sanctuary. Terrified of the number 13, Ethan had always avoided anything associated with it, but fate had led him to this cursed place.

As Ethan cautiously ventured deeper into the forest, he heard the distant echoes of chanting and ritualistic drums. Ignoring the gnawing fear in the pit of his stomach, he pressed on, compelled by a morbid curiosity to uncover the source of the sinister sounds.

Finally, he reached a clearing shrouded in darkness, where hooded figures danced and swayed around a blazing bonfire. In the center of the clearing stood a stone altar, upon which lay a sacrificial victim, bound and gagged.

Frozen in terror, Ethan watched in horror as the cultists raised their voices in unholy praise to the number 13. With each chant, the air seemed to thicken with malevolent energy, and Ethan felt the suffocating weight of dread pressing down upon him.

Suddenly, the cult leader, a sinister figure cloaked in black robes, stepped forward and locked eyes with Ethan. Sensing his fear, the cultists seized him and dragged him toward the altar, their twisted faces contorted with sadistic glee.

Bound and helpless, Ethan could only watch in horror as the cultists prepared to enact their dark ritual. With trembling hands, they raised a gleaming dagger, its blade glinting in the flickering firelight, poised to plunge it into Ethan's heart.

In a desperate bid for survival, Ethan struggled against his bonds, but it was futile. With a final, blood-curdling scream, the dagger descended, and Ethan's world was consumed by darkness.

The cult of 13 had claimed another victim, adding to their grim legacy of terror and death. And as the echoes of their twisted chants faded into the night, the forest reclaimed its secrets, leaving only the chilling reminder of the darkness that lurked within.

Similar phobias

1. Number 4 (Tetraphobia): Common in East Asian countries like China, Taiwan, and Japan, buildings often skip floor numbers containing the digit 4 due to its resemblance to the word for "death" in Classical Chinese. Similarly, Nokia's mobile phone series avoids model numbers starting with 4.

2. Friday the 13th (Paraskevidekatriaphobia): Widely considered a day of bad luck in Western cultures, it's also feared in Greece and some parts of Latin America. In Greece, Tuesday the 13th is also regarded as unlucky.

3. Number 17 (Heptadecaphobia): In Italy, the number 17 is often avoided because in Roman numerals it can be rearranged to form "VIXI," meaning "I have lived" but interpreted as "I am dead." Thus, some planes and hotels skip row or room 17.

4. Number 39 (Triakontenneaphobia): In parts of Afghanistan, the number 39 is believed to be cursed or associated with shame, possibly due to its association with thirteen times three.

5. Numbers 616 and 666 (Hexakosioihekkaidekaphobia and Hexakosioihexekontahexaphobia): These phobias stem from the Biblical "number of the beast," 666. The number 616 is also feared due to its association with this Biblical concept.